RIVER
ADVENTURES

GANGES

W

This edition published 2015 by
Franklin Watts
338 Euston Road
London NW1 3BH

Franklin Watts Australia
Level 17/207 Kent Street
Sydney, NSW 2000

Design, editing and picture research by Paul Manning
Maps by Stefan Chabluk
Proofreading by Alice Harman

Produced for Franklin Watts by
White-Thomson Publishing Ltd

www.wtpub.co.uk
+44 (0) 845 362 8240

A CIP catalogue record for this book is available from the British Library.

ISBN 978 1 4451 3931 9

Dewey classification: 915.41'1

Note to Teachers and Parents

Every effort has been made to ensure that the websites listed on page 32 are suitable for children, that they are of the highest educational value and that they contain no inappropriate or offensive material. However, because of the nature of the internet, it is impossible to guarantee that the content of these sites will not be altered. We strongly recommend that internet access is supervised by a responsible adult.

Printed in Malaysia

Franklin Watts is a division of Hachette Children's Books,
an Hachette UK company
www.hachette.co.uk

Key to images

Top cover image: The Ganges at Varanasi
Main cover image: Hindu pilgrims on the Ganges
Previous page: A Royal Bengal tiger
This page: Bathing in the Ganges at Haridwar

Picture Credits

t = top, b = bottom

Front cover top, Shutterstock/Neelsy; Front cover main, Shutterstock/Luisa Puccini; Title page, Shutterstock/neelsky; Contents page, Dreamstime/Nike Sh; 4, Wikimedia/Rikkimaheshwari; 5t, Stefan Chabluk; 5b, Dreamstime/Jeremy Richards; 6, Shutterstock/Alexey Fateev; 7t, Dreamstime/Yekaterina Kirillova; 7b, Dreamstime/Aleksandar Todorovic; 8, Shutterstock/Orin; 9t, Dreamstime/Alexei Fateev; 9b, Dreamstime/Paul Prescott; 10, Dreamstime/Daniel Boiteau; 11t, Courtesy International Rivers; 11b, Dreamstime/Dennis Donohue; 12, Dreamstime/Izoneguy; 13t, Dreamstime/Daniel Boiteau; 13b, Dreamstime/Jayanand Govindaraj; 14, Wikimedia/Julijan Nyca; 15t, Dreamstime/Zatletic; 15b, Wikimedia/Fowler&fowler; 16, Dreamstime/Aleksandar Todorovic; 17, Getty/Mario Tama; 18, Dreamstime/Arseniy Chervonenkis; 19, Dreamstime/Steve Allen; 20, Wikimedia/Fowler&fowler; 21t, Dreamstime/Guido Vrola; 21b, Dreamstime/Zatletic; 22, Ritesh Maity; 23t, Corbis/Gideon Mendel for Action Aid; 23b, Dreamstime/Samrat35; 24, Dreamstime/Samrat35; 25t, Dreamstime/Arindam Banerjee ; 25b, Dreamstime/Orangeline; 26, Dreamstime/Ivan Stanic; 27t, Still Pictures/David Woolfall; 27b, Shutterstock/neelsky; 28, Dreamstime/; 29t, Still Pictures/Kiron Kha/Photo Bangla/SpecialistStock; 29b, Still Pictures/Joerg Boethling; 31a, Dreamstime/Ekaratch; 31b, Wikimedia/Einar Fredriksen; 31c, Dreamstime/Johnnydevil; 31d, Shutterstock/Ido; 31e, Dreamstime/Foodmaniac; 31f, Dreamstime/Paulhenk; 31g, Dreamstime/Isselee.

Contents

A Ganges Journey	4
The Ganges' Source	6
The High Valleys	8
A Fragile Land	10
The Upper Ganges	12
The Ganges Plain	14
Allahabad	16
Varanasi	18
Patna	20
The Farakka Barrage	22
Kolkata	24
The Ganges Delta	26
Life in the Delta	28
Glossary	30
Ganges Quiz	31
Websites and Further Reading	32
Index	32

A Ganges Journey

The Ganges is the longest river in India. It stretches for 2,500 km (1,500 miles). Fed by many different streams, it flows from the Himalayas in northern India to the Indian Ocean. You will follow the river from its source, through India and Bangladesh to the Bay of Bengal.

A life-giving river

For thousands of years, people living on the banks of the Ganges have relied on its waters for drinking, washing, cooking and watering their crops. The vast Ganges plain is one of the most fertile farming areas in the world. Its rice and wheat feed hundreds of millions of people.

▼ The Ganges plain stretches for 1,200 km (746 miles) across northern India. When the river floods, rich silt is left behind to feed the soil.

A source of water

Use of the Ganges for growing crops goes back to ancient times. Today two canal systems help to supply water to farms across the fertile Ganges valley. Because so much water is diverted, the river is less used for transport, but in West Bengal and Bangladesh farmers still use boats to take their goods to market.

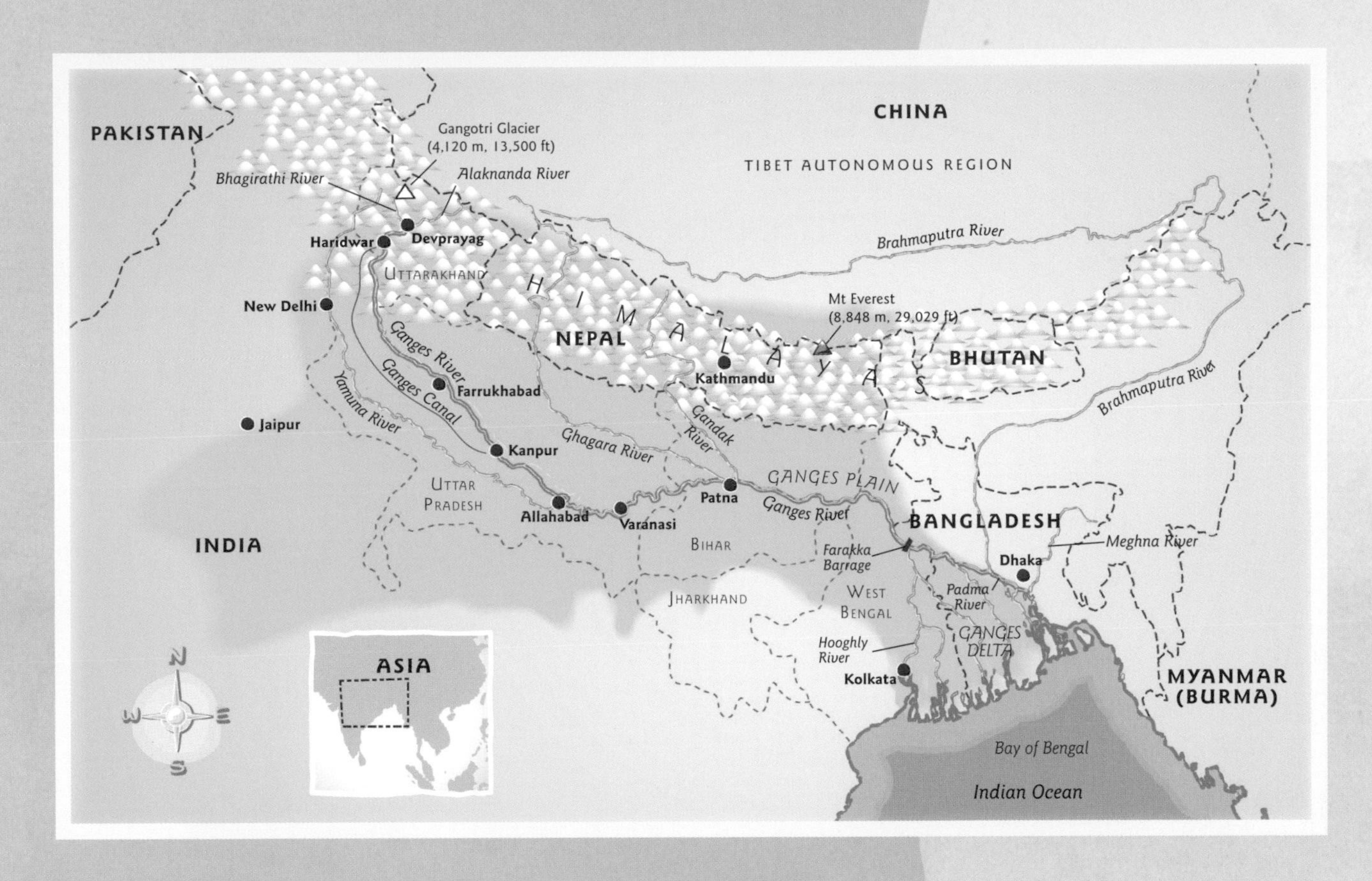

▲ Many rivers, known as tributaries, join the Ganges on its journey to the sea.

A holy river

For India's Hindus, the Ganges is a holy river. Its waters are believed to wash away sins. Every Hindu hopes one day to visit the holy city of Varanasi on the banks of the Ganges, and bathe in the river. Each year more than a million Hindus make this special journey, known as a pilgrimage.

▶ Washing, bathing and praying beside the Ganges is a daily ritual for millions of Hindus.

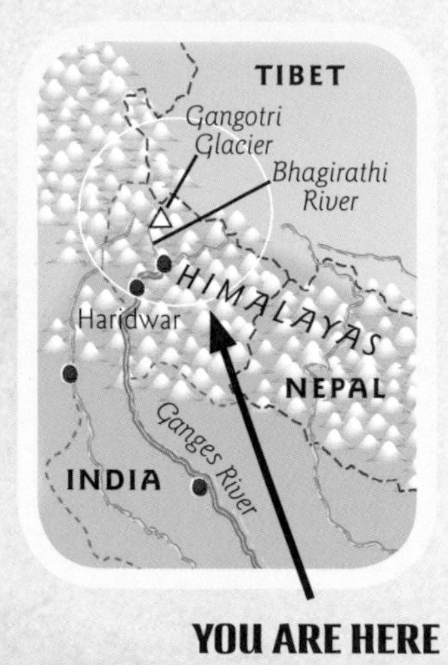

The Ganges' Source

The source of the Ganges is the Gangotri Glacier in the Himalayan mountains. Your journey begins in this remote area, more than 4,000 m (13,100 ft) above sea level.

▼ Snow-capped peaks tower over the Gangotri Valley in the central Himalayas.

On top of the world

The Himalayas is the world's highest mountain range. It stretches for nearly 3,000 km (1,864 miles) through Pakistan, India, Nepal, China and Bhutan. Around 100 million years ago, two gigantic plates of rock were pushed together by forces below the Earth's crust. Where they collided, the plates were forced upwards. This massive movement created the Himalayan mountain range.

◀ The Ganges' most distant tributary is the Bhagirathi River. It starts in this ice cave just below the Gangotri Glacier.

What is a glacier?

A glacier is like a frozen river. It is made from layers of snow which are packed down to form a dense mass of ice. The huge weight of the ice sets the glacier moving very slowly downhill. Over thousands of years, the movement of the glacier carves out a wide U-shaped valley through the mountains.

Earthquake!

Underneath the Earth's surface, the same powerful forces that created the Himalayas millions of years ago are still at work today.

Sometimes the pressure from below makes the earth tremble in a violent jolt called an earthquake. Fortunately, most earthquakes in the Himalayas take place away from towns and cities, but in October 1991 a massive earthquake struck the town of Uttarkashi near Haridwar. It destroyed 42,000 homes and killed more than 1,000 people.

◀ This Hindu holy man has walked hundreds of miles to visit the source of the Ganges and bathe in its waters.

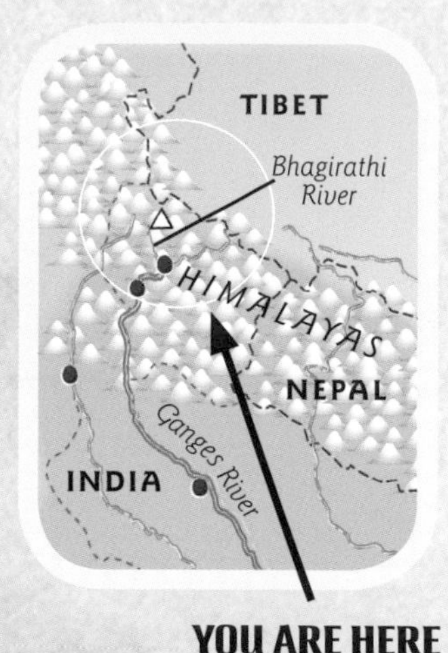

The High Valleys

In the Himalayas, life is hard. The land is covered with snow and ice for half the year. On your journey downriver, you meet the people who live here and farm the land.

Terraces

To create flat land for growing crops, the farmers create level areas called terraces and build stone walls to hold back the soil. The terraces collect rainwater and help to prevent soil from being washed downhill during the heavy monsoon rains.

▼ *This Himalayan hillside has been terraced so that the land can be used for growing crops.*

◀ In spring and summer, meltwater and monsoon rains pour down from the mountains to swell the Ganges.

The monsoon

Northern India lies in the path of seasonal winds called monsoons. The monsoon season comes when the winds blow inland from the Indian Ocean. These winds bring tropical rainstorms that last for days and can cause heavy flooding. Around 80 per cent of all India's rain falls during the monsoon season.

The rainy season

Between November and February there is little rain, and the Bhagirathi flows slowly. By March, the air begins to get warmer. Snow and ice start to melt in the mountains. This meltwater swells the river. In late June, the heavy monsoon rains arrive and the river becomes a raging torrent. Sometimes it rains so much that the river bursts its banks and floods the land.

▶ A Himalayan farmer collects feed for her cattle.

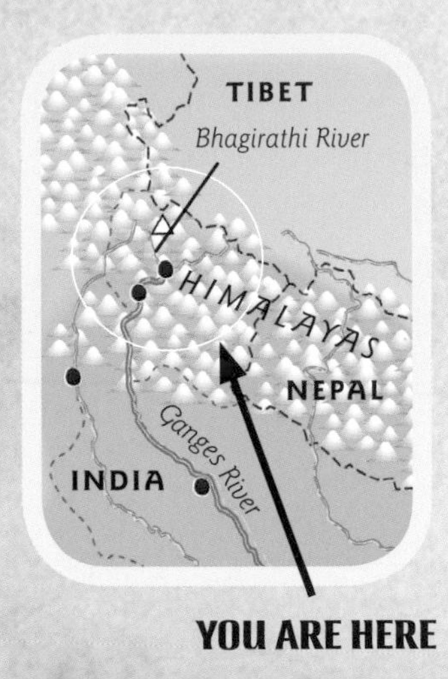

A Fragile Land

On the lower slopes of the Himalayas, forests are cleared to make way for roads, houses, mining and farming. Trees are also cut down for firewood. In places, you can see bare soil where the land has been stripped of trees.

▼ The Bhagirathi River winds through the Himalayan foothills. Because of human activity, the forest that once covered these hills is disappearing.

Vanishing forest

In mountain areas, rocks and soil are constantly worn away by the weather. This is called erosion. Usually erosion takes place very gradually, but when trees are cut down, the soil is suddenly left exposed.

With no tree roots to hold it together, the soil is quickly washed away by rain and ends up in the river. This raises the water level and can cause flooding.

▲ This hillside has been damaged by illegal dumping of mining waste.

Protecting the forest

The villagers of the Himalayas are often blamed for cutting down trees. But fuel is scarce and other choices, such as paraffin, are expensive. People also need land to build houses. Farmland is too precious to use for housing, so forest is cleared instead.

Some villagers have set up tree nurseries to replant areas that have been deforested. Environmentalists are also working with local communities to develop other sources of fuel, such as biogas and solar power, so that fewer trees need to be felled.

Wildlife at risk

When forests are cut down, many wildlife habitats are destroyed and animals become endangered. The forests of the Himalayas were once home to tigers, leopards, rhinoceros and deer. Today, these animals are found mostly in special protected areas or nature reserves.

◄ Because of habitat destruction, Himalayan species such as the snow leopard are in danger of dying out.

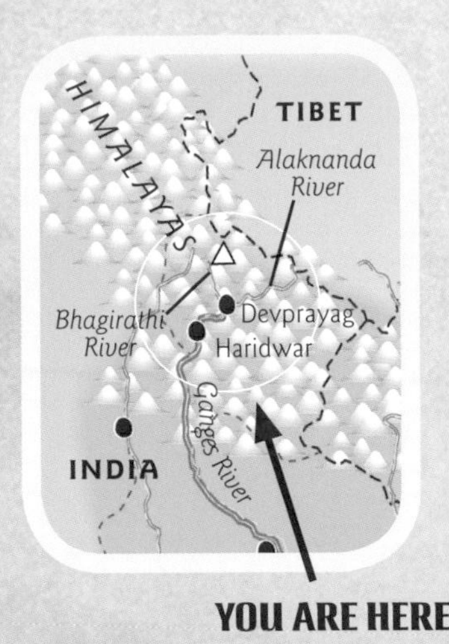

The Upper Ganges

Heading down from the mountains, the Bhagirathi races over rapids, waterfalls and through steep canyons. The roar of the water is deafening!

Devprayag

On its journey, the Bhagirathi is joined by other rivers. The largest tributary is the Alaknanda, which meets the river at Devprayag. This town has become a place of pilgrimage for Hindus. From here onwards, the river takes the name Ganges, or 'Ganga'.

▼ *Because of its fast-moving current, the Upper Ganges is a favourite area for whitewater rafting.*

◀ At Devprayag, the Bhagirathi River meets the Alaknanda. The name Devprayag means literally 'holy meeting of the rivers'.

Where rivers meet

The place where two rivers meet is called a confluence. For Hindus, any confluence is sacred, and the meeting of the Alaknanda and Bhagirathi at Devprayag is a holy place. The river banks here are lined with stepped platforms called ghats. Pilgrims use the ghats to bathe in the waters of the Ganges.

A haven for wildlife

South of Devprayag, you follow the Ganges through Rajaji National Park. This area in the Himalayan foothills was created to protect the landscape and its wildlife. The thickly wooded park is home to 50 types of mammal, including tigers, leopards and elephants, as well as nearly 400 bird species.

In the middle of the river, four islands lie within the park boundaries. These are a rich habitat for wildlife. As you set up camp for the night, you can hear hornbills calling to each other in the trees above.

▶ At Rajaji National Park, elephants come to the river to drink and bathe.

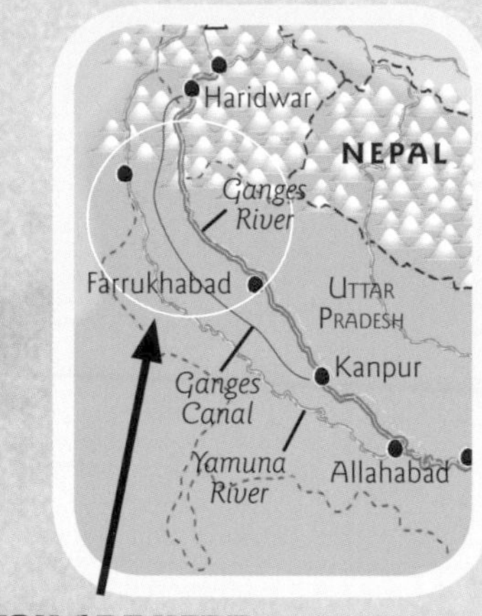

The Ganges Plain

At Haridwar, the Ganges leaves the Himalayan foothills and flows across the Ganges plain. This area is almost flat, so the river moves more slowly now, except in the rainy season when the land is flooded.

▼ *With its rich soils, the Ganges plain is one of the most fertile and densely populated farming areas in the world.*

Farming the floodplain

Throughout the Ganges plain, people live in small villages surrounded by fields of rice or wheat. Compared to Europe or America, the farms are tiny – about the size of two football pitches. Many farmers grow just enough food to feed their family. Others grow crops to sell in local markets. All these people depend on the Ganges River and Ganges Canal (*see opposite*) to water their crops.

◀ A farmer and his son plough their fields with the help of a team of oxen.

As India's economy grows, young people are leaving country areas to find better-paid work in the cities. Farming methods are changing too, as farmers use chemicals to help grow more crops.

A pollution blackspot

You reach the industrial city of Kanpur, 138 km (86 miles) from Farrukhabad. Along the riverbanks, factories called tanneries pour harmful chemicals into the river. This pollution is a real danger to people further downstream. The Ganges also contains high levels of untreated sewage, so you must be sure to boil and filter any water from the river before you drink it.

The Ganges Canal

Between the Ganges and the Yamuna rivers, the Ganges Canal runs for 900 km (560 miles) through the state of Uttar Pradesh. The canal supplies water to the area known as the doab, *or 'land between the rivers'. It also acts as a store for surplus water that falls during the monsoon season.*

▶ The Ganges Canal was built in the 1850s. Today it supplies water to nearly 9,000 sq km (3,475 sq miles) of farmland.

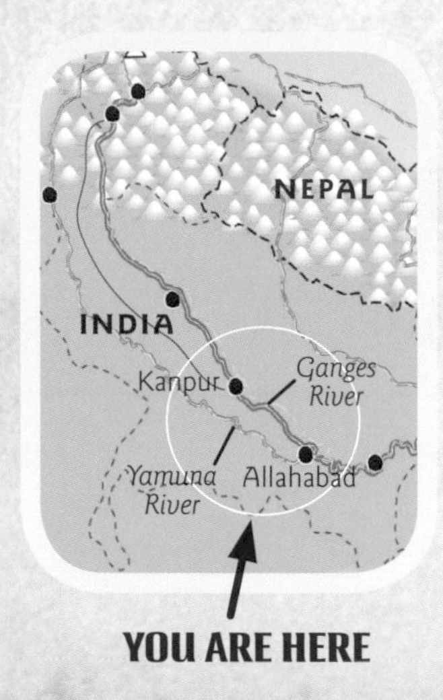

Allahabad

About 200 km (125 miles) from Kanpur, the Ganges and Yamuna rivers meet at Allahabad. This ancient city was founded more than 4,000 years ago. Its original name, Prayaga, means 'meeting of the rivers'.

A city of pilgrimage

Allahabad is a city of over one million people. Originally, it was an important strategic site, and anyone who ruled it also controlled the rivers. Today, many farmers gather here to sell their crops. The city's main industries are cotton manufacturing and food processing. For Hindus, however, it is above all a place of pilgrimage. Many thousands visit it every year to worship and pray beside the Ganges.

▼ *This vast city of tents houses the millions of pilgrims who visit Allahabad during the Hindu festival of Kumbh Mela (see opposite).*

▶ Hindu pilgrims bathe in the Ganges during the 2007 Kumbh Mela festival.

Kumbh Mela

The festival of Kumbh Mela is India's biggest Hindu gathering. At the last Kumbh Mela held at Allahabad in 2013, more than 100 million pilgrims took part, making it one of the largest gatherings of its kind in history.

At the climax of the festival, huge crowds gather to bathe in the river and chant the words 'Long live Mother Ganga'. Pilgrims also pray, listen to sacred music, give gifts of money and food to the needy, and receive blessings from priests and holy men.

A third river

At Allahabad, Hindus believe that the Ganges and Yamuna rivers are joined by a third, underground river called the Saraswati. It is named after the Hindu goddess of knowledge. Ancient Hindu texts mention the Saraswati, but it has never been found. It may have been part of the Ghaggar, a dried-up river which now only flows during the monsoon season.

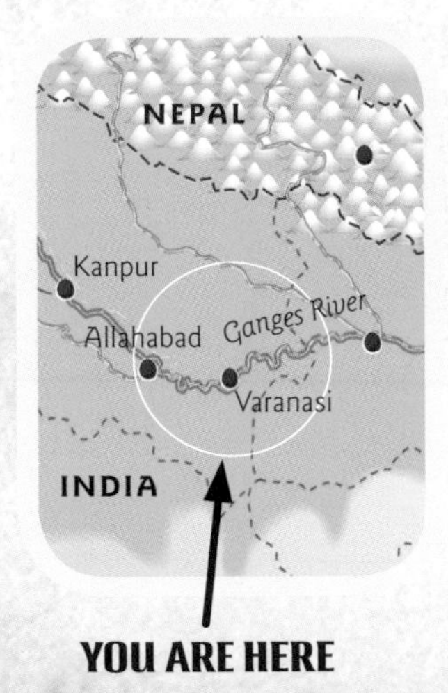

Varanasi

About 125 km (72 miles) east of Allahabad, your journey brings you to Varanasi. During festival times, this holiest of all Indian cities is packed with pilgrims, and the noise, colour and activity are overwhelming.

▼ *Varanasi is a holy city. Hindus believe there is a special path to heaven at this part of the Ganges.*

'City of Light'

Varanasi's location on the Ganges makes it very special for Hindus. For most of its course, the river flows south-east, but at Varanasi it suddenly bends north. On the west banks of the river, the ghats face the rising sun. At dawn, these flights of stone steps are crowded with priests, pilgrims and others who come to the river to pray.

A Hindu funeral

At the Manikarnika Ghat, a group of mourners are attending a Hindu funeral. After the body has been washed in holy water, it will be burned on a pyre of sweet-smelling sandalwood. The family will then scatter the ashes on the Ganges.

The old city

Leaving the river, you head into the old city and wander through a maze of narrow alleys where shops are selling silk souvenirs. Varanasi is a centre of the silk industry and is famous for its beautifully coloured fabrics. Other important industries here are toy-making, jewellery and metalwork.

River burial

Hindus believe that when a person's ashes are scattered on the Ganges, his or her soul will go straight to heaven. Because of the risk to health, the Indian government has tried to stop people cremating bodies beside the river, but it is hard to make them give up ancient customs, and the practice still goes on.

▶ There are about 100 ghats at Varanasi. These stepped bathing areas stretch for more than 6 km (4 miles) along the river.

Patna

About 260 km (161 miles) from Varanasi, you reach Patna – the capital of Bihar state. This historic city was once the capital of an empire covering nearly the whole of India.

A historic crossroads

Patna began as a small fortress overlooking the Ganges. A city grew up around it, including palaces, a university, gardens, temples and markets. Today, Patna sprawls for 16 km (10 miles) along the south bank of the Ganges. As well as a centre of rice-growing, Patna is a major river port and an important crossroads for people travelling to and from the north.

▼ The Mahatma Gandhi Setu is a bridge which links Patna in the south to northern Bihar. At 5.5 km (3.4 miles), it is one of the longest river bridges in the world.

◀ Rice needs a lot of water to grow. These rice fields are fed all the year round by monsoon rains and water from the Ganges.

Patna rice

Leaving the city, you visit some of the rice-growing areas in the surrounding countryside. Rice was first grown in India around 5,000 years ago. It is the country's most important crop. In many villages, you see people at work in flooded fields called paddies, harvesting the rice by hand.

Much of the rice grown here is consumed at home. One variety, basmati rice, is an important export. Between 5 and 6 million tonnes of basmati rice are harvested across India each year.

A vital food

Because most Hindus do not eat meat, rice is a vital part of people's diet. Most Indians eat rice at least once a day. About 600 different types of rice are grown, and rice-growing is a source of food and income for around 50 million Indian households.

▶ This woman is planting rice seedlings grown in a nursery field.

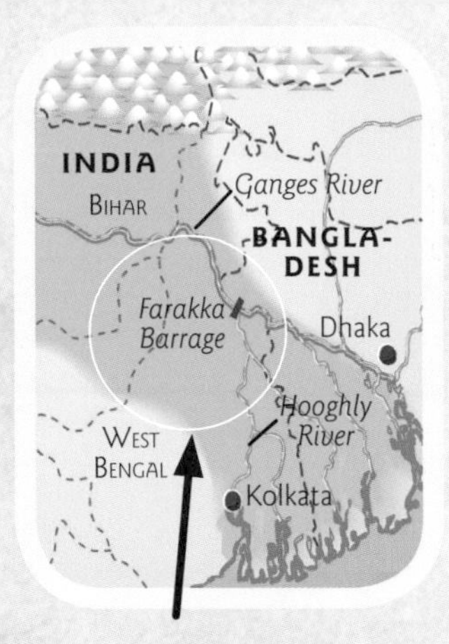

YOU ARE HERE

The Farakka Barrage

Near the border with Bangladesh, the Farakka Barrage stretches across the river. This huge dam was built to divert water from the Ganges, so that big ships could travel up the Hooghly River to Kolkata.

A controversial dam

When the barrage was built in the 1970s, it caused great anger. Bangladesh accused India of stealing the Ganges water. Since then, the two countries have shared control of the dam. This partnership is important to both countries. As their populations rise, more and more people in India and Bangladesh rely on the river for fresh water, food and transport.

▼ The Farakka Barrage is one of the longest river dams in the world. It is also a road bridge for cars and trucks.

◀ While some areas are affected by drought, others suffer catastrophic flooding. In Bihar, floods caused by heavy monsoon rains regularly swamp homes and farmland.

Whose water?

Because of climate change, water shortages in India and Bangladesh are getting worse. Currently, India is planning to divert more water from the Ganges to drought-affected areas of Uttar Pradesh. If the plan goes ahead, it is certain to lead to more trouble between India and Bangladesh.

Effects of the barrage

Since the barrage was built, silt from the river has become trapped behind it, and the level of the riverbed has steadily risen. Because of this, some low-lying land in Bihar is now waterlogged all the year round.

The dam has also stopped fish from reaching their spawning grounds, and several species that once lived in this stretch of the Ganges have disappeared. Because of this, many local fishermen have lost their jobs.

▶ Fishing is a vital industry for people living by the Ganges. Carp, catfish, mullet, freshwater eels and prawns are all caught in the river.

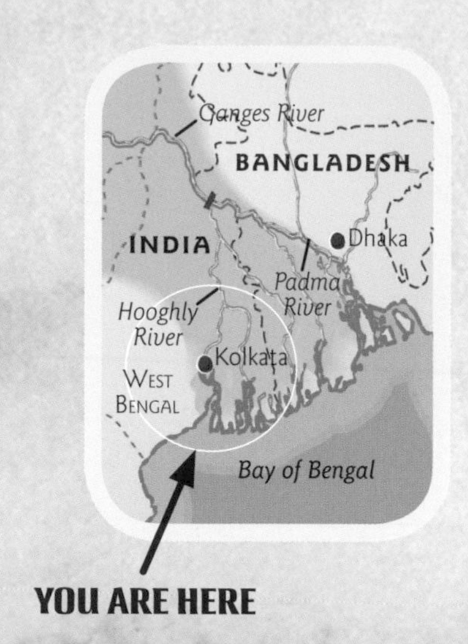

YOU ARE HERE

Kolkata

From Bangladesh, you cross back into India to explore the Hooghly River, which flows south towards Kolkata.

A river port

With a total population of more than 18 million, Kolkata is one of the most densely populated cities in the world. Its streets are choked with traffic of every kind, from cars, taxis and bicycle rickshaws, to farmers carrying their produce to market in carts pulled by oxen.

Three hundred years ago, Kolkata was the gateway to east India. For 80 years, it was India's capital. Today, it is a fast-growing commercial, industrial and financial centre, and a major port.

▼ Rickshaws carrying passengers and goods crowd the streets of Kolkata.

◀ The Howrah Bridge connects Kolkata with its twin city Howrah on the opposite bank. More than a million pedestrians use the bridge each day.

A Bengali city

Because of its river and coastal position, Kolkata has always been an important port. Goods made in India are shipped from here all over the world. Under British rule the city was known as 'Calcutta'. In 2001 it changed its name to Kolkata, to reflect its importance as a centre of Bengali culture.

Rich and poor

With the arrival of new industries such as IT and electronics, wealth is returning to Kolkata, but many of its people are still desperately poor. Around a quarter of a million Kolkatans live in overcrowded slums, without sanitation or clean water. Many earn a living by searching the city's rubbish dumps for things they can mend, clean up and sell.

▶ Bengali cooking is hot and spicy. These tasty fried snacks called pakoras are being cooked and sold at a Kolkata street food stall.

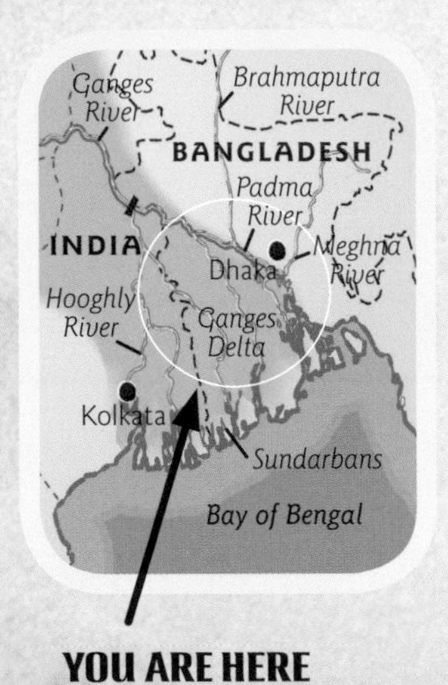

YOU ARE HERE

The Ganges Delta

Back in Bangladesh, the Ganges is joined by the Brahmaputra, to form the Padma. This river is wide and slow-moving as it winds its way to the sea.

A land of silt

Over thousands of years, silt dropped by the Ganges, Brahmaputra and Meghna rivers has formed a vast area of marshy land, called a delta. The Ganges Delta covers 130,000 sq km (50,100 sq miles), an area the size of England. It is the largest river delta in the world.

▼ Small boats crowd the river at Dhaka, the capital of Bangladesh.

◀ These Bangladeshi villagers live in makeshift shelters of bamboo and straw. They have no water supply except the rivers where they wash themselves and their animals.

Crowded Bangladesh

Bangladesh, where most of the delta is situated, is a crowded country that faces huge challenges. Most of its people live in small villages on low-lying land, where they are in constant danger from floods and tropical storms. The soils of the delta are good for growing rice and jute, and people live by catching fish. But in rural areas there are few schools and hospitals, and many people are very poor.

The Sundarbans

Criss-crossed by narrow waterways, the Sundarbans are the largest mangrove swamps in the world. Many animals live here, including rare birds, spotted deer, tigers, crocodiles and snakes. In Bengali, the name Sundarban means 'beautiful forest'.

▶ The endangered Bengal tiger lives in the Sundarbans, a strip of swamp and forest that stretches for about 270 km (167 miles) across the delta.

Ganges River
Brahmaputra River
BANGLADESH
Padma River
Meghna River
INDIA
Dhaka
Hooghly River
Ganges Delta
Kolkata
Sundarbans
Bay of Bengal

YOU ARE HERE

Life in the Delta

As you explore the delta's maze of narrow rivers, you meet the people who farm and fish here. Many live on shifting islands barely a metre above the tide. They are at risk from floods and cyclones, as well as from rising sea levels.

▼ These delta boatmen are running a ferry service for villagers. There are few roads here, so rivers are the main transport highways.

Fishing the delta

With so much land taken up by sprawling cities, the rivers here are a vital source of food. Most of the catch is freshwater fish, but some fishermen travel further out to catch shrimps and other types of seafood. These are exported to Japan, Europe and the USA.

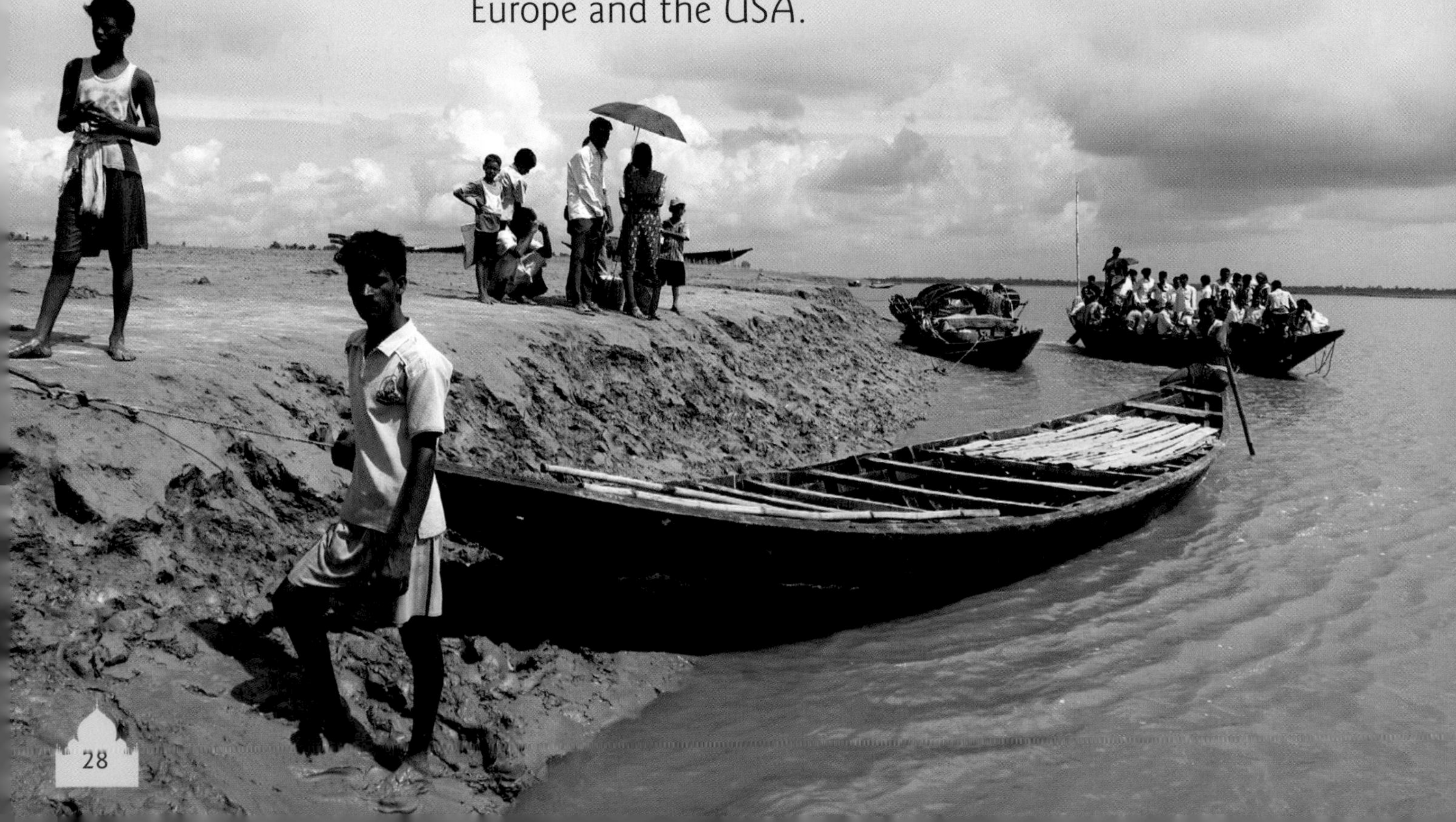

◀ Farmers cut down jute stalks in a field. Once harvested, the tough jute threads are woven together to make sacks and rope.

Climate change

Farmers of the delta need the annual monsoon rains to wash away salt and restore the soil. But too much rain can ruin crops and destroy livestock and homes.

As sea levels continue to rise as a result of global warming, the future of the delta and its people is uncertain. Experts say that sea levels could rise by as much as 0.5 m (1.6 ft) by 2100. If that happens, much of Bangladesh could end up under water.

Surviving the floods

In Bangladesh, villages are gradually becoming better prepared for floods and other natural disasters. Many now have specially built cyclone shelters where people and animals can be safe during storms and monsoon floods.

▶ This concrete storm shelter is built on stilts to raise it above the floodwaters.

Glossary

barrage a type of dam used to control the flow of a river

biogas a type of fuel produced by rotting organic matter

canyon a deep, steep-sided valley

confluence a meeting of two rivers

consume to eat or use

cremation the burning of a dead body

cyclone a type of tropical storm

deforestation cutting down trees, e.g. for timber or firewood

drought a time when water is very scarce

dung waste from an animal

erosion the wearing away of soil or rock

fertile good for growing crops

floodplain the area affected by a river's floodwaters

foothill a smaller type of hill often found around, or at the base of, a mountain range

fragile delicate, easily harmed

ghat a stepped platform for bathing

glacier a slow-moving mass of ice

global warming the rise in the Earth's temperature caused by carbon gases in the atmosphere

gorge a steep, rocky river valley

habitat the natural home of a plant or animal

Hindu a follower of Hinduism, the main religion of India

livestock farm animals such as sheep or cows

meltwater the flow of water from melted snow or ice

monsoon a seasonal wind which brings rain

mourner a person who attends a funeral

nursery a place where plants are grown from seed

paraffin a type of fuel often used for heating

pesticides chemicals used to kill plant-eating insects

pilgrimage a journey to a holy place

pollution chemical or waste products that harm the environment

purify to cleanse or wash

pyre a pile of wood on which bodies are cremated

rapids a stretch of fast-flowing water

remote far away, difficult to reach

rickshaw a bicycle taxi

sacred holy

sandalwood a sweet-smelling wood used for cremation

sanitation toilets and running water

sewage human or animal waste

silt fine sediment carried downstream by a river

slum a run-down area where people live in very poor housing

solar from, or to do with, the sun, e.g. solar energy

source the place where a river begins

spawning ground a place where fish lay their eggs

strategic important for winning a fight or battle

tannery a factory where animal skins are turned into leather

tributary a river or stream that flows into another, larger one

waterlogged full of water

Ganges Quiz*

Find the answers in this book, or look them up online.

1 Match the captions to the pictures.

1

2

3

4

5

6

A A ferry boat on the Hooghly River

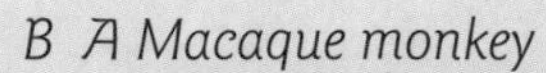
B A Macaque monkey

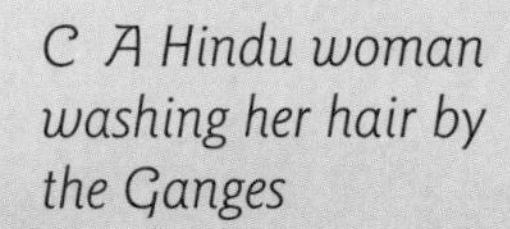
C A Hindu woman washing her hair by the Ganges

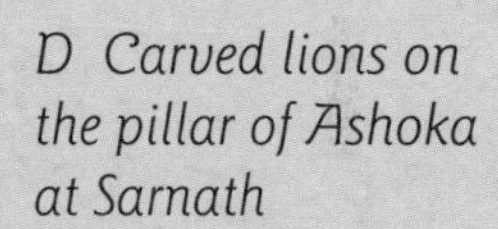
D Carved lions on the pillar of Ashoka at Sarnath

E Basmati rice

F A statue of the Hindu god Shiva on the banks of the Ganges

2 These places can all be found along the Ganges. Place them in order, starting with the ones nearest to the sea:

Varanasi
Devprayag
Farrukhabad
Patna
Kanpur
Allahabad
Haridwar

3 True or false?

'Bengal tigers are fierce when cornered, but hardly ever attack humans.'

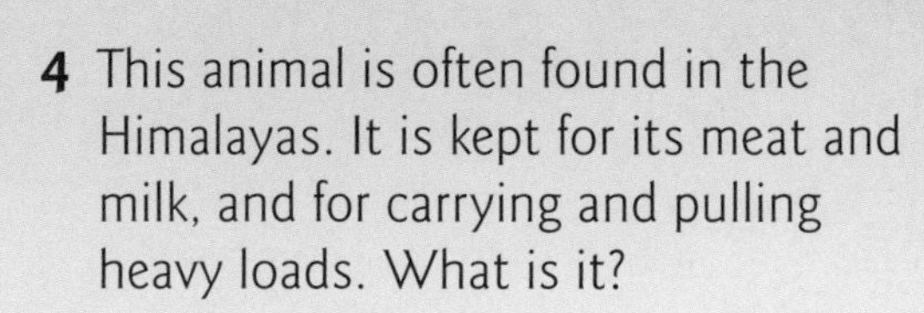
4 This animal is often found in the Himalayas. It is kept for its meat and milk, and for carrying and pulling heavy loads. What is it?

*Answers on page 32

Websites and Further Reading

Websites

- *http://kids.nationalgeographic.com/content/kids/en_US/explore/countries/india/*
  Good short introduction to India.
- *www.worldwildlife.org/species/ganges-river-dolphin*
  Fascinating facts about the Ganges river dolphin.
- *http://resources.woodlands-junior.kent.sch.uk/homework/religion/hinduism.htm*
  Useful background material on Hinduism.

Further reading

India and Mumbai (Developing World series*)*. Jenny Vaughan (Franklin Watts, 2013)

The Ganges: India's Sacred River ('Rivers Around the World' series*)*, Molly Aloian (Crabtree, 2010)

The Ganges ('Journey Along a River' series*)*, Paul Harrison (Wayland, 2009)

Index

Alaknanda River 12, 13
Allahabad 16–17, 18

Bangladesh 22–3, 26–7, 29
Basmati rice 21
Bay of Bengal 4
Bengal 25
Bengal tiger 1, 27
Bhagirathi River 10, 12–13
Bihar 20, 23
biogas 11
Brahmaputra River 26

climate change 23, 28–9
confluence 13
cremation 19
cyclone 28, 29
Dhaka 26

deforestation 10–11
Devprayag 12, 13
'doab' 15
drought 23

earthquake 7
erosion 10–11

Farakka Barrage 22
farming 8–9, 14–15, 16, 21, 28–9
Farrukhabad 15
fishing 23, 27, 28
flooding 9, 11, 14, 21, 23, 27, 28, 29

Ganges Canal 15
Ganges River
  a holy river 5, 13, 16–17, 18–19
  course 4, 18
  delta 26–8
  plain 4, 14–15
  source 6–7
  upper river 12–13
Gangotri Glacier 5, 6, 7
Ghaggar River 17
ghats 13, 18, 19
glacier 6–7

Haridwar 1–2, 7, 14
Himalayas 4, 6–7, 8, 10–11
  foothills 10, 14
  forests 10–11
Hinduism 5, 12, 13, 16–17, 18–19, 21
Hooghly River 22
Howrah Bridge 25

Indian Ocean 4
industry 16, 19, 23, 24, 25

jute 27, 29

Kanpur 15, 16
Kolkata 22, 23–4
Kumbh Mela 16–17

Mahatma Gandhi Setu 20
Meghna River 26
monsoon 8, 9, 15, 17, 21, 23, 29

Padma River 26
pakora 25
Patna 20–1
pilgrimage 5, 12, 13, 16–17, 18,
pollution 15, 19
poverty 25, 27

Rajaji National Park 13
rice 4, 14, 20, 21, 27
rickshaw 24, 25

Saraswati River 17
silt 4, 23, 26
snow leopard 11
solar power 11
Sundarbans 27

terracing 8–9

Uttar Pradesh 15, 23
Uttarkashi 7

Varanasi 5, 18–19, 20

water shortage 22–3
wheat 14
whitewater rafting 12
wildlife 11, 13

Yamuna River 15, 16

Answers to Ganges Quiz

1 1D, 2B, 3A, 4F, 5E, 6C. **2** Patna, Varanasi, Allahabad, Kanpur, Farrukhabad, Haridwar, Devprayag. **3** False. In Bangladesh, between 50 to 200 people every year are killed by tigers. **4** A yak.